Evolve

Evolve

The Lifetime Power
of Actions on
Your Career Path

Ydalmis Carrasco

NEW YORK

LONDON • NASHVILLE • MELBOURNE • VANCOUVER

Evolve
The Lifetime Power of Actions on Your Career Path

© 2020 Ydalmis Carrasco

Published in New York, New York, by Morgan James Publishing in partnership with Difference Press. Morgan James is a trademark of Morgan James, LLC. www.MorganJamesPublishing.com

ISBN 978-1-64279-460-1 paperback
ISBN 978-1-64279-461-8 eBook
Library of Congress Control Number: 2019901238

Interior Design by:
Bonnie Bushman
The Whole Caboodle Graphic Design

In an effort to support local communities, raise awareness and funds, Morgan James Publishing donates a percentage of all book sales for the life of each book to Habitat for Humanity Peninsula and Greater Williamsburg.

Get involved today! Visit
www.MorganJamesBuilds.com

To all my clients, who showed me the way.

Table of Contents

Foreword

We all need a little push every now and then. It may be a little push or a big push sometimes. Decision making can be a difficult task, particularly for women, and especially when other people depend on her like kids or parents for example. But even if that is not the case, taking a chance or a risk, deciding to change things in your life is a big deal, mostly because of the fear of failure. Evolve is a wonderful book to help you make a difference in your own life. The guide that will take you step by step in the process of decision making, taking action and responsibility for your wellbeing in both your personal life and your professional life. Ydalmis is great at motivating you to get things happening, to take action. Her personal story, told in a funny and genuine way, is exciting and should be taken as an example to set high standards for yourself. In Spanish we have a saying, *Nadie aprende por cabeza ajena*, which means that nobody learns from somebody else's experiences. But Ydalmis is betting on the exact contrary. She knows that her personal story may be a mirror in which so many women struggling to thrive and break barriers can look at themselves. The best part of this great book is the specific advice, the steps to identify what your need and what you want. And then the exact actions that will take you to that new path that will make you happy. In the end, if you want to make others happy, you have to start with yourself.

— **Celimar Adames Casalduc**
News Anchorwoman & Emmy Award Winner

Introduction

You got it! You have this book in your hands, and I'm hoping that you read it without stopping, like you are drinking your favorite coffee from Starbucks. Think for a moment that you have received an envelope with an invitation to meet your lifetime mentor who will guide you to choose between a job's new role and a lifestyle as entrepreneur. Imagine that it will set you apart from the rest of the world. This really happened to me! This book is full of challenges, fantastic stories, experiences from around the world, and *one* final action that will make you stronger to make the decision of your new professional life. Once you go through every page of this book, you will realize that the possibilities are closer than you think and that there are thousands of women like you who found the way, like me. You have the power and the responsibility to choose wisely!

All the stories I will share with you during this journey will make you laugh, think, cry, and even pee in your pants sometimes, but, my friend, they are the *truth!* Every action that you will follow here has a specific reason, and it is structured in a way that will allow you to control your own steps. Let's say that you are in a stage of recognition: you stop in front of the mirror, and what you see is good, but not great. I'm talking about your self-awareness. If you get a dictionary, you will probably find a meaning similar to this: "conscious knowledge of one's own character, feelings, motives, and desires." It is not just physical but internal readiness to face the world out there.

Now is time for you to look around and find a good, comfortable spot and be by yourself (*shhhhhh*, don't tell anyone). Think about having the opportunity to ask for clarity, to find a map with the right path and the key to a door that goes beyond your desires. Start asking yourself these questions: What is that fire inside of me that can't be extinguished? What keeps me awake during the night? Why haven't I made it happen yet? Those types of questions are the ones that will take you closer to those dreams that have been in the back of your head for years. Now it is time for you to reactivate them and put them in motion.

That is why I'm writing and why I do what I do. I want to help you to get where you want to be, and then it will be easy for you to make the decision that will bring you stability and self-confidence. You will also succeed faster than you can expect. I have been traveling around the world, working for so many years in corporate and coaching women from different countries. The corporate ladder is a great school, providing you with a lot of resources, building your character, and preparing you to be a better professional with competencies, skill sets, and empowerment. On the other side, entrepreneurship is a world of uncertainty but flexibility; you manage your own time, you can control work-life balance, there's more time for you and your family, and other priceless perks. But what about finding the sweet spot?

Oh my goodness! you may be thinking, *these are the same questions that have been on my mind for years.* Find the best of both worlds. Early in my career I was focused on my growth: how fast I could pass every learning curve, how many positions I could achieve, how much money I could make. That is wonderful for a twenty-two-year-old. At that time, you can have the privilege of being wrong, confused, or even take some short cuts on your personal development, and that's fine! What I can tell you is that you can see yourself through my story, talking about tough times, struggles, depression, and feeling angry, scared, inadequate, unstable, those type of emotions are the ones that at the end give you the power to move to the next stage in your journey. I will also show you what it will take to be whatever you want to be. You will know who I am and where I'm coming from. To be honest, I will also tell you some secret weapons for you as a woman that can't be missed.

I have so many friends, clients, and peers who ask me almost every day, "How can I manage different responsibilities and have the clarity to identify new opportunities, have the right network, and move in the direction that will really take me closer to my desires?" Every one of you has the same resources that I have, but do you believe enough in yourself? Do you think that you can find the way to get in to the best career path? My dear reader, you really must tie your shoes and start running this marathon with me, because I was on the same path that you are on now. Believe me, it was easy when I found my coach and she took me under her wing. If you can make the decision and say yes to yourself, you will be unstoppable! This is what I did. Every time I struggle or have a moment of uncertainty, my first reaction is asking myself, "What is next?" The evolution behind that question is the results of many nights thinking, "What if? Where can I find the guidance or someone who can show me the way?"

At this moment, I'm so happy that I want to celebrate with you the awakening of your new life! You are reading what I really want to share with you, and during the next pages you will see what I'm talking about. Let me give you a great example of how I was feeling when I was in your shoes. I was confused, and sadness was part of my limitation. There was so much that I wanted to do, but at the same time, I was not sure what the right thing to do was. The first step in the plan was to open my heart and be honest with myself. The answer was inside of me, but I didn't know where to go for resources or even to find the right person who would help me to start a new journey of my new me. The internet is a great tool of course. Google is one of my cool friends, and searching will help to find programs, tools, assessments, websites with different alternatives to how you can find the real deal on your future plan. My second step was to start reading more about my passion. I watched videos, I got some trainings, I registered in some personal development programs, I went to conferences, and I met some interesting people and expanded my network, but all of that was not enough to make the *big* decision on my career path.

I've been in both worlds—in the corporate job and the entrepreneurial life—and I will define in this book every action that you have to take to move forward. I have friends everywhere around the world who make me more knowledgeable, but at the same time, I opened my eyes, so I could be that independent woman with the self-confidence to look beyond to the possibilities.

When you understand that you have the power to control your own destiny and that you're ready to step up, that is the moment when you start shining. It is in your hands. You are the only one who can take yourself to the other side and live the professional life that you deserve. The time is *now!* Start speaking your truth, and with all the tools that you will find here, you don't have to reinvent the wheel. I did it first for you, and I will make it easier for you as well. My mission is to help you to surpass all those difficult moments, to make you stronger, to attract the impossible, and to be the successful woman that is in you. If you are a woman you are a leader, that is the first part of the game and you are winning already! We don't have to be identical, but, my friend, our efforts together are going to change the world. What I can say here, for your eyes *only,* is that repetition is the mother of perfection. Don't tell anyone, but that is the secret sauce. The rest of the humans on this planet will be amazed by your transformation, because when it's coming from your heart, everybody will notice it. When God created you, he did it in a way that was completely perfect, the same way that He wants for your life. Come on! Wake up and smell the coffee. It is about time. The reality is that I'm writing from my heart. You will know everything about me, at what time I go to bed, if I brush my teeth, what is going on behind the scenes when I'm getting ready for an interview, how I deal with motherhood—you'll know it all! The action steps that you will follow here are going to be your treasure. No more hunting, baby! The professional woman, independent and international, has come here to stay and will be brave enough to conquer the universe. I want to be your ambassador, the one that makes you feel like you are a *powerhouse!* Follow me and read the whole book. I guarantee you that when you finish, we will be *pro*-besties (professional friends).

Blessings!

CHAPTER 1

Lost and Found

How many times has something happened and you didn't understand the reason why? For example, you are late to go to a medical appointment or to a meeting and you lose your keys, or maybe your phone doesn't have much battery on your way out and you don't know where the power cord is. Does that sound familiar?

Everything in life happens for a reason. The key here is having the capability to take it the way that should be. Stop for a second and say to yourself, "It's fine. I will find the keys or the power cord, and if not, then I will change my appointment or inform them that I will be a few minutes late." If you don't do this, then you will feel angry, disappointed, and in a bad mood. But if you control your situation at that moment, the rest of the day will be fine or even great.

Do not get lost like your keys. I know that feeling. The problem resides in how you can control facing the obstacles in your life with a better attitude. I've been lost, too, and being lost is a horrible sensation. Here is another way to experiment with the sensation of losing something or someone. Imagine that you're shopping, and your daughter decides to hide in the middle of the clothing rack. You call her, but she is playing and doesn't want to answer. What do you do? This has happened to me. In that moment, I want to cry or scream. I was mad at myself and I felt disoriented; it was awful!

Yes! You have been found! If you are here reading this book, it is because you know that a piece of the puzzle is missing. The good news is that you ordered this book with a specific intention. You are looking for guidance, and you want something different in your life. You don't know how, when, or who is going to help you.

Let's start with part one: the assessment. I want you to ask yourself the following questions, as this will help you be in a better position to find clarity. They are simple questions, but the answers are going to determine what is next.

1. Tell me something interesting about you.
2. What is the most important moment of your life?
3. Where do you see yourself in six months?
4. What is your favorite country?
5. Do you want to be famous?
6. What book did you recently read?
7. Why did you buy this book?
8. How long ago did you meet your oldest friend?
9. Who is your favorite person from a movie?
10. What type of drastic change do you want to implement in your life?

After these questions, it will be easier to see where you are. The best part is that you must show the answers to me! Promise that if one day I'm on the stage giving a talk and you see me, you *better* talk to me and let me know what your story is after reading this book, OK? Promise?

Some of the women out there are lost or disappointed, and they can't even speak about their desire of being in a better place and being safe.

My mission is to find as many women as possible, help them, and wake them up to move forward in their lives! I want you to keep going and let the woman in you be the one that makes this process move forward.

All of us have a voice inside that keeps telling us, "What are you going to do?" "I'm waiting for you to do something different," "When is the day that you are going to make the decision?" and "Let me get out of here!"

I want you to be clear in your professional career and in your personal life. First, be clear with yourself. This book is your resource for getting on the right track and moving in the right direction. Each one of the following chapters is going to have a very specific objective, and most of them will be opening different doors to lead you to the answer for the big decision: climb the corporate ladder or become an entrepreneurial woman? Get ready!

It is your choice!

CHAPTER 2

My Story

Imagine a two-year-old girl coming from a communist country. That was me. My parents were smart enough to leave Cuba in 1970 to look for a better life. My father had to work for the government for almost two years before we left the island, and every twenty-eight days, he was released to come home for two days before going back to the sugar cane fields.

I remember his stories. He was a hard worker, and he knew that there was only one way to get my mother and me out of that country. My mother was pregnant with me and lost her job due to having submitted a request to leave. One day, the government came to take our house, leaving us homeless. In that moment, we were facing the new reality of our life until the day that we received the news. We were authorized to migrate, and the claim was approved—our dream come true! We immediately talked with rest of the family, and we went to the airport with just one suitcase for the three of us and the illusion of a new world. I was sick because my hemoglobin levels were very low. To find meat and food in Cuba was very difficult, and that was the main reason why my parents decided to move out of that tumultuous and horrible way of living.

My father, Jose, the oldest of five children, was the right hand of my grandfather. At the young age of eight, he was selling vegetables around his neighborhood to bring money home for the rest of the family. His education was very short-lived, but he was smart, agile, and ambitious.

My mother, Alminda is the sweetest woman in the universe, the oldest and the only girl in her family. When my brother, Alex, and I were growing up, my mother was very tough and strict. If we disobeyed her rules, the consequences were dire. We both went to a Catholic school run by nuns. As you can imagine, our environment was very disciplined but full of love.

During school vacations, my "summer camp" was working with my father. When I say "summer camp" it is because nowadays our kids have the opportunity to go and have fun during their vacation. For a lot of us, our summers were about learning life lessons, having new responsibilities, and growing in a mature environment that made us better citizens of the planet. My father had a cafeteria where I washed lettuce, counted the pennies, and talked with customers. It was fun. I remember that I was so excited to wake up at 4:00 a.m. to buy the provisions and the rest of the supplies to start our day at work. I showed my report cards to the clients, and they left some tips behind. That was the best part. I learned the meaning of work ethic, responsibilities, and commitment, three words that are part of my parent's life philosophy.

At the age of fourteen, I had my second job. It was in a department store working in the kid's clothing area. One day a lady asked for the layaway section, and I didn't have any idea what she was saying. I was confused, and once I discovered that it was about different payment terms, I got my first layaway item as well. It was for my brother, Alex. Of course, that's what happens when you love your siblings and think about them before yourself. Every two years, I was ready to move to the next job to learn more and increase my earnings.

I graduated from high school with honors, and I was one of only two students who were accepted to the University of Puerto Rico (UPR), the most prestigious college in that country. I studied mass communication, with a concentration in advertising and public relations. During my days in college, I had an internship in Arvelo Advertising, an agency that showed me how to work around men, be ready for the unexpected, and look all the time for better opportunities.

On the other side, I had a part-time and very exciting side line job: I was a character on TV. If you are from Puerto Rico, you probably remember *Entrando por la Cocina con Luisito Vigoreaux.* I was the long rice, Cinta Azul, or "Cintia," in a kitchen show. *Oh my goodness!* That character was a very important part of my life for almost five years during college. She taught me how to be whoever you want to be, how to face everything with enthusiasm, how to love people, and how to be authentic. I was also doing TV commercials as a main talent for coffee, paint, cigarettes, shampoo, and sangria, among others.

My life has always been so exciting since I was very young, meeting people from every country, having opportunities to be financially stable, and of course going through tough times before, during, and after different stages of my life. Imagine, when I was nineteen-years-old, a friend of my mom called me to let me know that she found a promo in the newspaper for a contest that she wanted me to participate in. It was Miss Puerto Rico Petite, and one year later, the crown was part of my story! Yes, I won! Holy macaroni! The unexpected happened: during that year, I won Miss Talent Show, Miss Friendship, and best of all, Miss Congeniality, like Sandra Bullock! She is one of my favorite characters from Hollywood.

Once I finished college, I worked at a multinational company, experiencing the fantastic world of telecommunication. I was the number thirty from all the employees of Cellular One, the innovator of the wireless world. Even when I liked what I was doing in customer service and sales, my desires led me to want more. Almost three years later, I got married, and I was hired by a great company in the pharmaceutical industry, where I have been working the last two decades of my professional life. That was a huge milestone; I was coming from communication and entering the science world

My real schooling was during those first ten years, when I belonged to one of the best Fortune 500 companies in United States. In those days, I learned everything about how to determine who your advocate is, who your mentor can be, and how you can bring quality of life to others in need. My first company was Merck Sharp and Dohme. It has the best new hire training that you can experience; the methodology, the accountability, and the empowerment that you acquire during the first three months of induction is second to none. I've been exposed to three different areas within the healthcare industry: pharmaceutical, medical device, and biologics. I have worked in more than twelve different leadership roles; managed around fifteen therapies, including the oncology market; and overseen twelve countries in Latin America, twenty-two islands in the Caribbean including Puerto Rico, and domestic positions in the United States. Traveling around the world during the past twenty-plus years has been crucial in increasing the scope of my professional life, in developing my potential, and in teaching me to choose what the "perfect" decision in the right moment is.

What I can say to you is that no matter your career path at this stage of your life, you must embrace what you have and look forward on what you really want for your future.

Keep reading because here we are going to work together to create your new you and set you apart from the rest of the world. I will explain in the rest of the chapters how I did it and what actions, adventures, challenges, and opportunities are part of my success today.

I know that you face challenges in your professional life and that you want to move upward on the corporate ladder, or you want to be your own boss but do not know what the best way to go is. I've been in both scenarios, and I can tell you that if you follow my actions here, you will find the right career path.

In 2001, I became entrepreneur. It was one of the hardest decisions that a single mom can make, but I was strong enough to open a kid's clothing store of a brand that was originally from South America and create a new profile in customs due to a foreign company and brave enough to continue with the economic challenge of opening on the same day as the tragedy of 9/11. What a year!

Let me tell you the story of how I became the owner of this first business. I was traveling very often to Argentina due to my scope of work and responsibilities. I was pregnant at the time and went to a shopping mall during my free time and found the store Mimo and Co. I bought some clothing for my baby, Sergio. I was in love with the brand's design and the line in general. Almost two years later, I asked myself, "What about having that store in Puerto Rico?" At that time, I was living on the island where one of the biggest malls of the Caribbean is located. I started my communication with the owners of the store—it was a family business with more than one hundred stores in Argentina. My store was the first one coming out of Argentina, and it was very intense not just to get the approval from their side but also to get the business loan and the authorization from the mall for me to be one of their tenants. Once they both say yes, I immediately put my business plan in action. I called all the parties involved and made meetings without stopping. I'm talking about planning with the architects and learning about systems and process from US customs, tax exemptions, POS systems, textile regulations, fire department permissions, government women entrepreneur aids, and multiple agencies to coordinate a successful launch of my store! Everything is possible, but you have to make it happen.

You are getting closer to learning more about how I did it and how you can make it. My story is not an extraordinary one, but I can tell you that what I did during the last two decades is going to help you to see yourself in my life.

Listen, I want you to make the commitment deep in your heart and promise yourself that this is it: you are going to start a new journey that will surpass your own goals and make the decision to invest in yourself. I want to say something more here before you jump into the actions in the next chapters. If you are a woman, if you have kids or are planning to have them, let me tell you something: Baby, you have the strength to do whatever you want. My dear reader, don't give up!

CHAPTER 3
The Actions

When you see the word *structure*, is that something that stresses you out? Or does it do the opposite—make you feel under control? This is what you are going to do forever, so just follow me on this. In any growing company, it is important to provide guidance and clarity. As a professional, you must always think about a formal structure early in the growth stage, regardless of whether you are an entrepreneur, or you are climbing the corporate ladder.

Let's start describing why you must be organized and structured. My routine starts around 5:45 a.m., but the night before I organize my clothes and the clothes of my kids and check my agenda to be ready as soon as the alarm goes off. I get ready, drive to my daughter's school, eat breakfast there, and move forward with my responsibilities, appointments, and, of course, time for myself.

Wait, I want to share a secret here; sometimes, I hit the alarm twice to stay in bed at least five more minutes. Is that familiar? These types of routines must be closer to who you are; they must match with your personality. Do not let your routine control your day; on the contrary, it will set the tone to make you happy and more productive and help you check off every task in your agenda. What I'm trying to say here is that the structure of your life is the baseline of your productivity and your success in the real world. It will be the mirror of your professional and career path. Here are at least four of the most important steps on your daily routine. If you start your day following these simple steps, the actions you are going to take in the rest of the chapters will help you have clarity and move in the right direction.

First step: on your way to work, make a plan in your head of ways to start the day on the positive side. For example, open the door for someone, smile to others at least twenty times in the morning (count it), give a compliment, or even stop at a bakery store to buy some pastries for a client, for your peers, or even for the kids at school. The satisfaction that you receive is priceless, and more people are going to see the kindness in you. You are going to have a great start full of positivity and energy.

Second step: open your agenda or calendar. You need to have everything scheduled, personal and work related, so be sure that you include time for lunch or to do something that gives you relief at the end of the day. Read all the emails in your inbox, delete what you don't need, unsubscribe from the unnecessary ones, and prioritize what to respond to.

Third step: you have to challenge yourself on a daily basis to improve and get better with what you really feel passion about, to have new goals, and to be ambitious with short- and long-term plans. If you can have a timeline to see your forecast planning, it will be amazing!

Fourth step: you must be connected every day with God, the universe, or whatever source you believe in. I must tell you that if I'm not waking up every day in a grateful state of mind, thankful and looking for his blessing, I can't be here writing to you today. Be connected!

The actions that you are going to implement through this journey are going to create a lifelong infrastructure that once you put in motion will have you asking, "Why didn't I do this before? Why didn't I hire a career coach years ago?"

No worries, my love. The time has come and the boss lady in you is experiencing the first feelings of the superpower-woman CEO. I know how you are feeling in this specific second; I was there! This is so cool! I'm happy for you.

This is what is going to happen: we are going to work with your mindset, education, skills, network, roles and responsibilities, personal development, financial stability, and more. Every chapter is created with a very specific purpose and is a proven method that works for me through the years. The measured risks that you will manage, that will take you to the next level.

Do you know how many women like you want to have the desire to be in her power, to manifest her goal, and to have the abundance and the professional career path that are part of their dreams? Millions of women are looking for their voice to be heard. They are looking for a better life, and professional stability. You are not alone. Let me tell you a story for you to have a better understanding of what other women out there want.

Once, I was traveling first class to Barcelona. Sitting next to me was a beautiful woman. Let's call her Ani. We talked for almost five hours, and she told me everything about her life in a snap shot. She was coming from a very rich family and had everything that she wanted during her younger years, but she hadn't finished college. Ani was fifty-four years old, had two young kids and never get married. She was a single mom, super ambitious, and looking for her next opportunity in her career. Ani talked about her professional life. She got zero satisfaction from her job because she was missing the passion. She wanted to be part of something bigger, to help others, and have fun in her daily life.

The objective with this story is for you to take in consideration that there is another woman like you out there, waiting for the clarity to make the right decision in her career and leave behind the mediocre professional world that she is living in.

You need to tell someone about your desire, ask questions, and look for a role in your life that will provide the missing piece of your puzzle and the financial freedom that you deserve. If you choose wisely, your next move in your career –corporate job or the lifestyle of the entrepreneur—will be easier to plan. You will start living your best life now!

The next chapter is your first action. I want you to be ready, be strong, and make it happen.

CHAPTER 4

ACTION 1—
Are You a PRO Yet?

P robably when you were young, you dreamed about being famous or having a future that is related to your passion. Or maybe you even dreamed of having the best of both worlds: working hard but playing harder.

When I was young I applied to work at Disney, but they didn't hire me because I was not living in Orlando. I really admire Disney as an institution. In more than ninety years of its existence, the name of Walt Disney has acquired a special position in the world of entertainment. The brand has acquired several businesses and has continued to grow the ambit of its products and services. Even though so many years have passed, their latest version of their mission statement was created in 2013. I was always in love with Disney for so many reasons, and I've been close to their philosophy even later in my career. I received a certification from their institute in leadership.

What I want to show you here with this preamble is that sometimes with dreams, we don't know how we can be closer to make them come true. You must be closer to everything that is related to your passion, goals, dreams, and desires because the attraction that is behind those efforts is going to take you closer to your destination. When I decided to apply to a job or to get a course or a training related to what I love, the rest of the pieces started falling together.

The reality is that every time you find a way to invest in your personal and professional development the achievements are higher. I have a bachelor's degree in mass communication and two MBAs, one in marketing and the other in healthcare management, but education is just one part of being a "pro." My master's degrees were paid by one of the companies that I was working for in 2003. Some of my more than one hundred certifications have been paid for by the companies that I was working for and the others from my pocket—I would say probably 80 percent and 20 percent, respectively.

You need to step up! No matter if you have a bachelor's degree, an associate's degree, an MBA, an MD, a PhD, or didn't finish any degree at all, it is time to start investing in yourself. You don't have to wait any longer. It is a lot of certifications, classes, webinars, conference calls, courses, trainings, and more education programs that can contribute to your personal and professional goals. Let's start getting into the real world. When you finish high school, you are in the best position to choose what is next, imagine that you decided to go to college for three to five years getting classes. Just right there your professional life starts.

This is my example: when I was twenty years old, I moved from the sunshine star of the Caribbean, Puerto Rico, to the great state of Maryland that I love so much. I applied for an exchange student program. For one year, I was far from my comfort zone learning a new culture, knowing no friends, and getting used to different weather, a new language, and another set of processes on campus—not to mention that the food was different.

The good thing was that I was fearless. My parents were supportive in terms of letting me go. I remembered that they told me, "We don't have too much money, but at least we can give you five hundred dollars." In 1989 and for a college student like me, it was amazing. I started the process by myself, talked to my counselor, and in less than three months I was accepted in Towson State University! Woohoo! That was one of the best decisions that I made in my life.

I registered in five classes each semester and out of the ten, eight were elective classes. Ha! My purposes for being out of my country were first to learn a second language and secondly to survive as an independent young woman. I made it!

The second semester I was an expert. Of course, my first half was a total adjustment. The curriculum was full of cool classes like ballet, tap dancing, jogging, Spanish, and the concentration classes like TV production, journalism, and statistics. I was jogging at 6:30 a.m. in the middle of forty- to fifty-degree weather, recording my concentration classes and transcribing into a notebook to study from there, which was very hard because my English was at a beginner's level.

At the same time, I balanced my weekends taking the train to Washington, Pennsylvania, Connecticut, and even to New York. Yes, I was working after classes on campus, and my scholarship helped during my new adventure, so I could travel by train to those states closer to the university. I can tell you a lot of funny stories during the days abroad, but let's concentrate on you for now.

The moment that you separate your feelings and cut the umbilical cord from your hometown is the moment you start getting ready for your professional life. Here are my two cents: graduating from college is a tremendous milestone, and if you did it, congratulations! Kudos to you for the effort and for running the extra mile. If you didn't, do not worry, I have good news for you. You better get back in the game. The next step is to secure your future; the following recommendations and actions are critical for you to deal with as you move forward with your life in your transition from college to career.

According to industry experts, the average number of times someone switches careers is four times. The way to identify the first step is by asking to yourself what your passion is about. The second step is asking what job can bring you financial stability.

The best example from my side is that I love art, but at the same time, I love science. I tried both during my college years and right after my graduation: first in the communication field and then, for the rest of my experience, in the healthcare arena. Once you recognize what moves you, then you must create the image of who you are. That means personality traits, energy, and characteristics that are part of your strengths, skills, and talents. Now is time to put everything in order:

First: take an assessment; the "Clifton Strength" in the book *Strengths Finder 2.0* by Tom Rath can introduce you to the power and potential strength that you have.

Second: open an account on LinkedIn.com. You can find me there; I have thousands of connections in my network that will really help you to apply to different jobs. Connect with people who are in the industry who you would like to work with. Search for human resource officers, recruiters, professionals who are decision makers, managers, directors, and even VPs. Contact then with a small note but be sure that you have a premium subscription. At least pay a monthly fee for access to "In-mails." Here is an example of a very effective note:

> *"Dear Mr. Smith,*
>
> *I'm pleased to share with you my career path and let you know that I'm looking for new opportunities. Some of my qualifications that can contribute to your company are a bachelor's degree in mass communication and two MBAs (marketing and healthcare management), twenty-three years' experience with communication,*

commercial operations and marketing for companies in the US, UK, Dutch and French Caribbean, Dominican Republic, Puerto Rico, and Latin America. I have sales experience in more than twelve countries with different cross-functional teams. I also have strong relationships around the region and launch experience with breakthrough brand, new products, and new segments extensions. I have capabilities as a leader of a team working in a multinational environment. I also have excellent communication and presentation skills, knowledge of political dynamics in Latam and in other regions, for example Europe, the United States, and Asia. I have the ability to network effectively both internally and externally. I'm fluent in English and Spanish. I can send you my résumé and marketing results so you can get a better understanding of my career path for the last two decades. You'll see that I have extensive management and operational experience that allow me to apply my skills in different areas as a Business Development and a commercial and marketing executive. Thank you for your time and consideration.

Best Regards,
(your name, contact number, and email)"

You need to send this note at least to fifty people for a five percent response.

Once you start moving and looking for a job that satisfies your needs and expectations, it is easier to choose if you are ready for the industry that you are applying for, or if you have a timeline to move to a second position within a year in the same company, or even if you want to try a different industry. At the beginning it's easier to change, because you are in the experimental mode. But if it feels right, stay with the company as long as you can. You are in a learning curve of a new position and new experience in the corporate world, so you want to prove yourself competent and develop a solid skill set.

My first job in the healthcare industry lasted for ten years, and I was promoted and changed to five different roles, one every two years. I had responsibilities in various cross-functional teams to have a better business perspective. In the corporate ladder that is a nonnegotiable aspect. You better learn the internal culture, departments, procedures, policies, and the most important asset and be close to the people. If you stay at least three to five years with the same company, you earn the respect from internal stakeholders and from external scouting from your consistency. Take in consideration if you work for a small company that is striving to grow and become self-sufficient that this is one of the opportunities to learn a lot, as most of the time you are working on stuff that in a big company is done by multiple departments and teams.

If you decide to leave the corporate world and move to the entrepreneurial life, I can tell you that I've been in both worlds, and they are fantastic. I really enjoy the benefits from each. This is what will help you the most as an entrepreneur: your mindset is one of the keys that works behind the scene to deal with the emotional part of being away from the corporate structure and the financial stability. It is time to create your own structure and prepare your bank account to face those moments of investment and other transitional expenses. Implement a routine of four basic steps into your day:

One: read an article or a book or find a source that is related to your field to keep you informed.

Two: meditate, pray, and create a mantra about your vision to be closer to your desires on a daily basis.

Three: write in a journal and get into a flow of gratitude. Release what is not working and manifest your goal.

Four: do at least fifteen to thirty minutes of exercise that keeps you in a good shape, emotionally and physically.

Your agenda and schedule must be your "bestie" from day one. Don't get lost, be ready for cancellations and changing appointments, and, most important, have at least one activity scheduled that makes you feel productive and brings happiness to your day. Now that you have a small taste of what is fundamental to be ready right from college for your first a job and how to expose yourself to the professional world to see if the corporate atmosphere is right for you (or not) we can move to the next action, which is related to the different hats you must wear and responsibilities you will have within your personal and professional paths.

I really enjoy my days now that I can see my life from a different perspective. If you truly want to have a solid career, you must have multiple experiences at big companies, start-ups, and small businesses. The last could be your own.

CHAPTER 5

ACTION 2—
Many Hats and Stages

Are you overwhelmed? Have too much in your plate? Losing focus? Been there, done that! But the difference is that I take it with a positive attitude. I will divide this chapter in two areas: the first is the perspective from the feminine side and the second from the professional.

To be successful in corporate or in your entrepreneurial life, this is how you tackle multiple roles and responsibilities. As a woman, you are already equipped with the "multitasking gene"; if you can put on your lipstick while you are waiting in a red traffic light, answer the phone, and reach for your kid's blanket on the back seat of the car, my friend, let me tell you that you are hired to be the best professional and successful woman out there. You will receive the golden medal of "Yes, you can." If you have in your mind two different ideas—one to move to higher position in your company and also your dream about creating a business that you are passionate about—don't wait any longer. It is possible!

Managing multiple projects may seem like a daunting challenge. Fortunately, there are several resources and strategies to help you stay on track and make it happen. I know that the demand as a woman in the modern society is overloaded, but the bright side is that if you set your priorities, don't procrastinate, work smart, and play harder, life is going to surprise you back. Work-life balance is critical. How many of us can really find that the sweet spot where you reward yourself on daily basis? It is important that you find that balance between work, family, friends, hobbies, and personal goals. Here are some tips that are going to contribute to bringing back your inspiration and the focus on your personal and professional development, and yes, they can coexist.

Go now and open your phone—unless you have Alexa at home, then you can use your virtual assistant—and look for your notes. Organize your to-do list for the week and make it real. Write down no more than *five* very important tasks from Monday through Friday that as a professional woman you must complete on a weekly basis. For example: check trends in the market of your industry, regardless of whether it is from the company that you work for or from your own business. Google trends from the United States or United Kingdom that are very reliable. Be open to reprogram and accept changes every day. You can arrange the agenda for the week. Sundays are the days that I organize my week, and, of course, my calendar is open for flexibility. In the calendar (Outlook) or on your physical agenda, schedule your personal side with errands, kids' activities and medical appointments. I have my calendar by color, so I can identify my personal from my professional to-dos.

One more thing you can do is open your heart to a new era and be social! When I say social, I mean both virtual and face-to-face social. My face and personal brand are in Facebook, Instagram, and LinkedIn. Today most of the people who have their own businesses are also on those platforms to generate leads and to expose and expand their network. Before you go live, you must believe in your message, in yourself, and in your brand. It is a lot of fun once you understand the benefits it can bring to your professional life.

If big companies entered in that space, why you can't do the same? The best way to increase your followers is by speaking the truth, being authentic, and being consistent. As women, we juggle so many responsibilities. We are mothers, sometimes single moms, and we have our careers, our friends, and our family goals. Some of us are the breadwinners of our homes and have other plans that we want to complete as well. This is key. Be fearless and take measured risks, because life is all about that.

If you are part of a Fortune 500 company and have an eight-to-five job, then this is for you. It is your responsibility to be committed, improve your skills, and get trainings, but more importantly, you must become a leader. I had the opportunity to have direct reports for years, and that is one of the most beautiful parts of working for a company where you can make an impact in the business but at the same time in other people's lives. As women leaders, we need to be ready to step up in the corporate world while we pursue our next position. This is one of the hundred other things that we can do to show others the impact that we can make.

In 2012, I received an award in recognition of growth, productivity, innovation, and people for exceeding results in projects and initiatives to Central America and the Caribbean region. The day that Novartis, the pharmaceutical company, gave me that award, I was very excited for the award, of course, but more than that, I was excited for the most important word in the recognition: *people.* At that time, I was pregnant, my job was more than one hour away from home, my salary was the only one supporting the household, my fourteen-year-old son was getting into a new school, and I was traveling every month.

So, my love, you can do it all. No excuses! I've struggled before. I've fallen and gotten back on my feet again. You can wear many hats in different stages of your life and shine brighter than ever before. In 2013, *Forbes* magazine published an article written by Anushay Hossain, a journalist from Bangladesh living in Washington, about women and multitasking. She wrote that "British psychologists confirmed what women have long known that we are, indeed, better at multi-tasking than men."[1]

Do you know how many times I've been on a phone call while brushing my daughter's hair, nodding my head to answer someone's question? Easy. It is part of our talents. I don't have to go that far to recognize that we are ready to embrace multitasking and be successful in each one of our responsibilities. Imagine, around 49.6 percent of the world's population is female, giving a total female population of around 3.52 billion in the world as of 2014.[2]

In conclusion, if you are a woman and a mother, that identity increases exponentially due to the awakening of our intuition and our "go get it" perpetual mode. We rock!

CHAPTER 6

ACTION 3–
Connect and Expand

The secret sauce of my network is to be connected to my mission: helping other women to step up and shine, one at a time. Once I create a connection with another woman as a coach, something inside of my guts keeps telling me the word *empowerment.*

I love social media. As you know, this electronic communication can create online communities to share information, ideas, personal messages, content, and even expand beyond international markets. After we are in labor at the hospital and you see for first time the face of your child, you look into their eyes, and it is like magic spell, the connection is immediate and forever. I can compare this with the way that social media have been connecting so many people in just one platform. It is easy to find someone who you have been missing for years, and it is a faster way to communicate with others. Facebook has 2 billion users, Instagram 800 million, and LinkedIn 500 million. That means that in terms of expansion, reach, and frequency, social media is almost a technologic miracle that can be translated directly to your business.

I've been exposed to every social media channel. The first time that I made my first live video in Facebook, the number of viewers was around two thousand. That was far more than I expected. I do at least one thing different every week, and sometimes more than five times per week. That helps me to have visibility, enhance the communication, and increase the number of members in my community. The usage of Facebook should be constant and daily to create awareness and credibility. I can tell you that is part of my success today. Sometimes I do interviews from women around the world. They tell their stories to be inspirations for other women who are probably watching. Other of my interviews are about specific topics; I post videos and articles, and I enhance my posts with links about business or inspirational stories. I even put pictures of my travels around the globe.

If you belong to a marketing department and you are working in corporate social media, you are creating social media websites and social media marketing techniques. If you have your own business, this ranges from small businesses and tiny entrepreneurial start-ups to mid-size businesses to huge multinational firms. There are a lot of benefits that you can maximize in your personal business and/or in the company that you are working for. You can:

- Create awareness of your personal brand
- Constant reminder for those clients who are connected 24/7
- Redirect your traffic to other pages
- Reach other market segments not usually organically reached
- Increase leads, create new partnerships, and retain old clients
- Enhance credibility and trust
- Spread the content faster
- Engage your audience on daily basis
- Offer interactive communication
- Generate metrics on audience behaviors
- Use targeted ads

- Keep close to the competitors
- For investment and a great source of ROI (Return of Investment)

I can mention thousands more benefits about social media for your brand. Personal brands or corporate branding, there's nothing like having your own experience with creating funnels, ads, boosts, or any other feature that you may find. A lot of people also contract services to create social media campaigns and have all the socials linked to each other. That is what I did: one of my best friends, Rosalie, is an expert in social media campaigns. We worked with my first "landing page" to generate clients, and it was connected to my calendar to schedule my appointments directly.

My recommendations for you are to be constantly connected, align your message with your brand, have consistency, and be yourself. That is why in my community, the posts, comments, and organic audience response are positive. I use those platforms for surveys, implementations, information, and business expansion. You increase your email data bank, and it is easier to develop campaigns with email blasts than any other communication vehicle. There are other social media channels that are important, but to start your business, choose two to three and be consistent with those until you have the number of followers that you want. Other social media channels are Pinterest, Twitter, Yelp, and YouTube. Remember that you can post live in Facebook and Instagram.

As a career and business coach, I can tell you that I really enjoy working with my clients and having the opportunity to be in constant communication with all of them. I can't do it without social media. The coaching sessions are sometimes face to face, but many of my clients are from different countries. I use Skype and Zoom for my meetings, coaching sessions, and interviews, and sometimes even to chat with my international friends.

Let me tell you my experience in LinkedIn that you should adapt:

- Connect with others who are in the same groups that you are
- Look for recruiters if you are looking for a job
- Post articles
- Share other people's posts
- Send in-mails to those who are in your same industry

- Get your profile to be 100 percent accurate and updated
- Use targeted words for others to find you on searching
- Let others know when you change your content
- Choose premium; the fee is very accessible
- Change the background of your profile
- Maximize the utilization if you are looking for leads, jobs, or connections
- Read the daily rundown weekly

There are so many recommendations that I can give you, but once you understand the benefits and perks that social media can bring to your own business or to the company that you are working for, it is easier to navigate. You will have fun with the results and analytics that you can find. If you start creating your own social media story and you need advice and support, my suggestion is to be in communication with the experts. The investment is just when your business or the corporate budget is ready to move to the next level.

Bloopers in social media are part of your learning curve. Going live is tricky. If you want to share the screen with someone else, you better practice for a few minutes or one day before at least from a different phone. If not, all your followers are going to see you, so please post the announcement of your live feed a few days before. That will help you to increase the viewers that day. It is important that you recognize when a person's comment is from a replay and when it is live, so you can answer in the comments knowing if they made it afterward.

Go and practice today, have fun, and be social!

CHAPTER 7

ACTION 4—
What Makes You Stronger

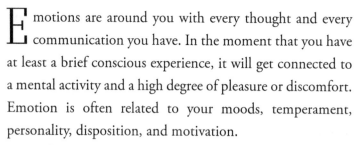

E motions are around you with every thought and every communication you have. In the moment that you have at least a brief conscious experience, it will get connected to a mental activity and a high degree of pleasure or discomfort. Emotion is often related to your moods, temperament, personality, disposition, and motivation.

Did you see the movie *Inside Out*? It is an animated movie about a young girl who has a wonderful life until her family moves to San Francisco and her emotions get out of control. How many times have you let your emotions control your day? Go and watch the movie and come back to this chapter. That will help you to understand ways to do and say things that sometimes are not under your control while others are easier to manage.

Your mental health can affect your daily life and your relationships and is also connected to your physical health. Mental health also includes the ability to enjoy and obtain balance between life events or activities and efforts.

Find happiness in your decisions, and when the day surprises you with something that was not part of your plan, embrace that moment and look for the positive side of it. Something that helps me relax and bring balance to my days is meditation, prayers, and journaling. Go and do something that you enjoy. We can have a hundred things to do, but if we don't face our challenges with positive thoughts, there's always going to be a moment that you complain, a moment that you feel uncomfortable, a moment of anger, and a moment of disappointment.

We all need balance between work and life. If you search for a work-life balance quiz online, you can probably find few for free. I recommend my clients take one of them: www.thepoductivityexperts.com. There are fifteen true-or-false statements for you to recognize if your life is in good balance. They also have twenty tips that you can take in consideration to live on balance, some of them are keep your sense of humor, take time for yourself, and learn to say "no."

Do you know what TED Talks are? You can watch them on YouTube, or even go to their webpage www.ted.com. TED Talks are one of my dreams: to be able to speak publicly on one of my favorite platforms. I've been in different stages, but TED is a nonprofit devoted to spreading ideas, usually in the form of short, powerful talks (eighteen minutes or less). TED began in 1984 as a conference where Technology, Entertainment, and Design converged. Today it covers almost all topics—from science to business to global issues—in more than one hundred languages. The exposure and the excitement to be part of the speakers with TED are priceless.

This is a great example of what can make you stronger. Once you identify in your life things related to your goals, you must prepare a plan toward that goal. Sometimes you have to do things related to your goal, that probably you don't like, and you have been trying to find the way to get there through a short cut.

I want to give you my point of view and what I did to avoid losing my time and getting on the right track. Those struggles or difficult times that you are facing are the strength of tomorrow. If you know Kelly Clarkson's song "Stronger," part of the lyrics are great for you to focus on your goal: "What doesn't kill you makes you stronger, stand a little taller, doesn't mean I'm lonely when I'm alone. What doesn't kill you makes a fighter..."

I got divorced when my son was almost three years old. It was a moment of truth. I was a stay-at-home mom for one year and after that year, my life collapsed in different aspects. That was when I said to myself, "No more depending on others." I had a great track record of achieving my goals before my thirties, and nothing stopped me from getting what I wanted after that. The moment when you become a single mom is crucial. You are fighting not for you, but for the love of your life—your child. I decided that I was the only one who could be the pilot of my new life and since that day I've been unstoppable; hundreds of projects and plans and my bucket list is infinite. Every year I go back to my resolutions, and I usually accomplish 80 to 85 percent of them.

You should embrace your life and get on the train of "Nothing is going to stop me." Today I have a great life. I have so many wonderful things that I'm grateful for, and those ones that made me struggle or made me cry, or those moments when I was living in scary city, they built my character and made me the woman I am today. The soul of being unstoppable is that you cannot be prevented from continuing or developing. You must feel that in your gut! Let me tell you what you are going to feel. You will not compete with anyone; on the contrary, people are going to compete with you. This is my recommendation:

- Your acts are going to come before the thinking process
- Your intuition is going to be right on the dot
- You will recognize that you can't control what is out your hands
- Your motivation is going to be your engine
- Never is going to be enough for you
- You must be honest with yourself
- Failing is part of the success
- Education and learning are ongoing processes
- Organization and structure are going to be part of your success
- Take measured risks and be fearless

Around the month of December 2017, the universe conspired to give me the opportunity to start a new journey. I've traveled to different countries that I hadn't visit before, one of them being Dubai, the largest and most populous city in the United Arab Emirates (UAE), on the southeast coast of the Persian Gulf. People call it "the land of yes!" One of the reasons why I was so excited to visit that country is because of the impact that has been created by women in leadership. The vice president and the prime minister of the UAE encourages women to participate in all sectors and created work environments that promote the equal participation in their development process. When you see other women around the world standing up stronger and making an impact in their environment, that is when you should open your eyes and make the course of your destiny.

How can we still be thinking about "What if?" No more! It is time for you to create your new way to move out the "hold on" for your goals. C'mon, let's move faster and dance with me! Oprah says to "surround yourself with only people who are going to lift you higher."

CHAPTER 8

ACTION 5—
Leaders Are Learners

What is a leader? Here is the definition from the business dictionary: "A person or thing that holds a dominant or superior position within its field and is able to exercise a high degree of control or influence over others."[3]

I would like to share with you a quote that is related to you. I wrote this quote and every time that I read it a lot of people come back to my memory: "A woman leader is capable to reach the impossible and carry her team to exceed their possibilities." Do you know how many women run the show in their country? And how many others are screaming to be out of their internal prison to let the world know about their desires and start creating their own empire? Are you one of them?

When you read social and demographic trends from Pew Research Center, you can see that one of the studies from the source Catalyst revealed that "women have made only modest progress in gaining top leadership positions in the business world. Today, 26 women are serving as CEOs of Fortune 500 companies (5.2%)."[4]

To get into a VP or CEO position in the corporate world requires a lot of effort and sacrifice and many years of experience to represent a woman in leadership positions. What we can do to be one of them? What does it take to have our business running from the same seat?

Women in top-level management positions today still face challenges. Some of those challenges are part of the struggles that we have to manage in order to move forward and faster. Let's do an inventory with eight different factors that are in the middle of our growth. These apply to your career regardless of whether you are working in corporate or you are your own boss:

- Reality check on salary and earnings discrepancy
- Lack of support from woman to woman as a one force
- Ask for salary increments

- Ask for continue education
- Follow a managerial skills development plan
- Lack of confidence to apply to C suite positions
- Be confident to speak up
- Take measured risks

The world is in constant flux, and as a woman you must be part of the evolution. We can stay in the same stage, stall, and lose time. It is part of our life's mission to be the force that generates the difference impacting other women's lives.

I want to empower your life by saying that if you don't feel like you have the power to make a life change, don't keep reading. But if deep in your heart you have the desire and you want to make 180-degree turn, this is for you.

You must let others know that you are ready to speak up, show them who you are, what your desire is, and then let the leader in you spread her wings. If you don't stop doing what you have been doing for the last ten years, my friend, let me tell you that you are going to be in the same position in ten more years.

Just think about it for a moment: go back in history and remember when in your life was the last time that you decided to do a drastic change or face a turning point that made a huge impact and people noticed it. It could have been a graduation, a wedding, childbirth, home ownership, travel out of the country, car ownership; any of these could be a major turning point that you experienced in your life already. Are you ready to be that woman who has the guts to declare, "Today is the day that I want to make my life and my dreams come true"? Can you stand up right now and look in front of the mirror and recite slowly from your heart each word here?

"I am a leader and, believe me, to become the leader that I am today was not easy, and I'm still under improvement. I will be forever. Even when you're born with those traits, it is your responsibility to feed them."

When I was six years old, my brother, Alex, came into my life. He was my first fan, follower, and almost my first direct report. He really embraced the idea of having a sister who is older, and that made the environment around him full of fun. It was not that bad, but I was very outgoing, expressive, and full of energy—and am still.

At school I was the first one in line or at my desk. I was the first one to say yes to all the activities and special projects. My grades reflected those desires. As a professional out of college, I wanted to always do something beyond my capabilities, and I knew deep inside of me that I wanted to do more. I always wanted to run the extra mile, and I challenged myself with goals that were almost impossible for a woman to reach.

If I look back twenty-five years, I was almost one of the thousands of women who didn't take the risks that I took. I'm telling you, *I am your girl!* You can be the woman who lives inside of your soul; together we are going to wake her up! In the moment that you came in to this planet the purpose of your life was written already. The situation here is that different circumstances put it on hold, but it is about time to turn it on.

Do you want to be part of the three to four percent of women who belong in the top-level positions in the corporate world? Or do you want to be the CEO of your company? At the end of the day, once you make the decision, you will start moving the needle in a different direction. To give you hope, yes! You can be part of either one.

CHAPTER 9

ACTION 6—
What Is Your Uniqueness

Talent is the best word to describe what is in you that makes you stand out from the rest of the people around the world. This a special ability and aptitude that you possess. You can do something without trying as hard. What is it? What do you have in you? Share with others your uniqueness.

In the Bible, the word *talent* is described in the New Testament in Matthew 25:14–30. This parable uses of the word *talent* to mean "gift" or "skill."

In 2015, the company Gallup conducted a study that showed that "about one in 10 people possess high talent to manage. Though many people have some of the necessary traits, few have the unique combination of talent needed to help a team achieve the kind of excellence that significantly improves a company's performance. When these 10% are put in manager roles, they naturally engage team members and customers retain top performers and sustain a culture of high productivity."[5]

There are certain characteristics that people with talent develop when they are in managing positions. It is part of their growth in their professional career path, and that makes the difference in their teams. Those characteristics are:

- People oriented (love to be around others, and make an impact in others' careers)
- Committed (don't count the hours in the office, the company is like their own business)
- Intuitive (it is easier for them to see beyond the problem; the solution is what they see)
- Risk takers (they measure the risk, but they are unafraid to take it)
- Motivated (they are natural motivators, they don't need someone to be motivated)

One of my favorite talents that I really enjoy is public speaking. I can talk in front of three people or thousands, and *I love it!* When I get in front of the audience and I see people's reactions, when I can bring happiness during that moment, when I make them think about possibilities, when I bring information that opens a new door of opportunities, or when I make a difference in their future and start our connection right there, creating a client who is ready to move forward in their personal and professional life, that's what makes my life complete!

My dear, lovely reader, if you have a talent that has been hidden, that is very special, that makes you unique, you must do something about it. We are women who are part of the world that is looking for a change. You should love to show others your skills and the gift that is part of the total package of who we are. Every time that you share your talent, you are helping other women do the same, and at the same time, your family, your friends, your peers, and everyone around you are going to be impacted. And guess what? It is your legacy, and that will remain from generations to generations. Coming from marketing, I did a SWOT analysis about my personality in business, and I want to share with you at least three characteristics of each area, so you can do the same. This what I found:

STRENGTHS	WEAKNESS	OPPOR-TUNITIES	THREATS
Communication and marketing experience	No time flexibility	Looking for learning something new	Other career and business coaches in media
US and international business exposure	When things are not done is unacceptable	Readiness for geographical expansions	Future trends
Structured	No patience for mediocrity	Business savvy	Changes in the entrepreneurial market

It is important to spend time with yourself and analyze who you are, have clarity on your strengths, and open your eyes for those opportunities that are around, because the weakness is something that you always can improve and for the threats, the only thing that you should do is watch them closer. Some of them you can't control. The market is very competitive; that is your baseline. If you have your own business or you are on your way to make that decision, you need to recruit people who are top talent, and you can attract the best candidates in the market, but you must be ready to do that first with yourself. The best experience comes from knowing how a recruiter engages with talent to find people that reflect you and your brand.

I had the opportunity to be part of different groups and boards that oversaw hiring new talents on the healthcare industry. I started interviewing people in 1997 and the evolution of the parameters and techniques have been changing dramatically. A few years ago, one of the ways to understand people's talents, skills, and experiences was through a first phone call to screen the candidate with questions that are very unrelated to the position or the role they were interested in. There are twenty-five questions that a recruiter or the hiring manager can ask you for your next role, here are just six of them:

1. At what age did you start working?
2. What do you like better, that people like you or that you like them?
3. How many hours of sleep do you need?
4. How many hours while you are awake are you in constant movement?
5. What are your hobbies?
6. Tell me about a project that you led.

You can use the same types of questions in your business when you need to start hiring people. Each one of them has a specific intent to find out more about the applicant and is related to loyalty, commitment, structure, and organization. When you must describe yourself or answer questions during the interview process is when you must demonstrate self-confidence even when you don't have all the answers. There is always a certain amount of uncertainty and anxiety during the process, but if you know yourself better and are prepared for that day, people can see your interest, and the talent will be recognized immediately.

Your uniqueness is the best strength that you can have. It is in your hands and the way that you show and tell others around you.

If you look the term *uniqueness*, in mathematics it is related to the phrase "there is one and only one." It is used to indicate that exactly one object with a certain property exists. It is the same about everyone in life, to stand out in the market you are one and only one who is going to make a difference with your own formula. Be bright, stronger, and conquer the world out there.

CHAPTER 10

ACTION 7–
Money–Attraction Mode

S how me the money! Go back into your story and think about your childhood and how money related to a stability factor. Was it a lack of resources or a pleasant environment due to the financial conditions that you were exposed to?

Research shows that having more money directly improves the development and level of achievement in children. Restricted income has a direct relationship with school outcomes and wider aspects of a child's well-being. Cognitive development and school achievement were most improved by having more money. Money seems to have more of an effect among low-income families than other socioeconomic statuses.

I remember that in my house, my parents both had full time jobs; they shared the expenses and provided everything that was necessary for each of us. We studied in a great private school, we had time for vacations, and every weekend we went to get ice cream and had friends and family over for get-togethers. My family worked hard, and we really enjoyed those days when everybody was at home watching TV and having dinner together as one. We were not rich, but our house was impeccable; there was always food in the refrigerator, and it was not that hard to make our monthly payments on time. My father worked in the restaurant industry for many years, and he always came back home with a lot of coins. He let me have some of them, but when we were growing up, it was very hard to ask for money that was not related to education and food. Entertainment was almost part of the no-no land.

Other factors that I found during my research were about educational outcomes that improved if mothers received additional money, like an extra income or having a side-gig, but not if fathers did. Some findings have direct relation and are consistent with a theory that predict that mothers are more likely to spend income on children than fathers are.

Is that incredible or what? My kids are affected by my decisions; they receive a certain amount of benefits and more opportunities when our incomes are stable. In the twenty-three years of my professional career, I've lost my job three times. My kids have been worried; they could feel the anxiety that my voice and energy brought into the house. When you must make a financial arrangement, immediately you must create a safe environment for your children.

The attraction that you create about money is part of the relationship that you have toward the abundance every day. You can find some meditations on money attractions in YouTube by Trigram Healing, the connection with God and the universe. In 2015, Steve Siebold, a contributor from *Business Insider*, published the results of the following article: "Interviewing over 1,200 rich people has taught me exactly how money affects the most important things in our lives." He found that "instead of seeing the positive ways that money can enhance the most important things in life like our health, family relationships, and friendships, most people would rather scorn money and tell you how it can destroy the things we hold closest to our hearts. Don't listen to negative people who don't know any better. The truth is money is not the most important thing in life, but it will make the most important things in life so much better."[6]

One of my favorite books of all time is *Think and Grow Rich* by Napoleon Hill. I have the audio version, and every time that I go for a walk or a run, I listen to the book. The book was written in 1937 for personal development and self-improvement. There are thirteen steps that include desire, faith, imagination, decision, the power of master mind, and the brain, among other very interesting content. One of the most important parts from that book is the persistence to believe in your desires and the potential to attract the income that you can imagine. I can say that money doesn't buy happiness, but it makes your life so much easier and provides the access to infinite opportunities.

I'm thankful and grateful to receive money. Because of money, I've had the opportunity to travel around the world, buy what I need and want—most of the time that includes my house, my car, and personal development certifications—support my family, and even provide beyond expectations.

Psychology Today published an article where the Gallup Organization, Princeton, and the University of British

Columbia conducted a study to evaluate if money can buy happiness and this is what was found: "The Gallup Organization asked thousands of people in 156 countries to rate their quality of life on a 0-10 scale, with higher scores indicating better life quality. The top 5 nations were all relatively wealthy, peaceful, liberal countries in which citizens had access to healthcare, family time, and education. Specifically, Denmark, Finland, Norway, The Netherlands, and Canada were the happiest."[7]

How is your organization with money? Do you like to reconcile your check book? Do you have a document in excel to track your expenses and earnings? If you answer yes to at least one of them, you are in the right track. If you want to be an entrepreneur and you can't manage your personal finance, you need your accountant ASAP!

Financial tracking is a process for monitoring cash flow. It allows you to not only monitor income and expenses, but to track how and where you are spending your money. It is a critical component to managing money because it gives you the big picture and creates a structure for spending. There are so many software options for financial tracking out there, and the majority are free. But if you don't want to invest, you can always go simple with your computer and save some money instead. There are also some apps for iPhone like Quick Books, Expending Tracker, True Bill, and Bill Tracking.

Money is great! You just must be ready to receive.

CHAPTER 11

ACTION 8—
Decision Time

R eady? Set? *Go!*
It is time to see all the chapters together and be ready to put in order a plan of action.

Decision-making is regarded as the process in a conscious way resulting in the selection of a belief or a course of action among several possibilities.

Every decision has a final choice, which may or may not prompt action. Decision-making is the process of identifying and choosing alternatives based on preferences and beliefs.

We have been talking about professional life, education, uniqueness, leadership, money, responsibilities, roles, and networking, and now it is time for you to start getting ready and continue with the new journey but taking in consideration that what you are going to do is for real and forever.

When we make a transcendental decision, it is imperative that an action plan is your guide and that you have a timeline with the specific days when you are going to complete the different stages.

This is the action plan that you should use; be creative, enjoy the process, and make it real!

ACTION PLAN—first template must be simple for you to start getting organized and have a better perspective on your plan.

Objectives: the purpose of the Action Plan; the number of objectives should match with each task.

Tasks: What do you need to do to achieve your objectives?

Responsibility: Who is going to be responsible for the task and support?

Metrics: How can you measure your success? Establish a baseline.

Time frame: Select a specific date to accomplish each task.

Resources: What do you need to complete the task?

Status: Add comments and follow-ups.

Today is a *big* day! You are in the final step to consider the results of your decision and evaluate what is better for your professional future. If the decision has not met your needs, you may want to go back a few chapters and think about the most important area of your life that is not aligned yet. This process takes time, but you know what is in your heart; it is just a matter of being strong and getting your mindset in the right direction to start the execution.

Some of the considerations for your decision-making is:

First: Recognize what is the best for you (corporate ladder vs entrepreneurial life).

Second: Identify your choices (position or role/type of business).

Third: Find testimonials cases that provide you evidence of success.

Fourth: Make some type of investigation, research, and comparisons.

Fifth: What actions you must put in place that help you to follow through.

Sixth: Use your action plan to organize your execution.

Seventh: Review everything and make the necessary changes.

After this process you will have a better perspective of your actual plan, and it will be easier to make some surveys to validate your decision. If you are in a corporate job, the organization and the structure will probably need to be more specific. If you are on the entrepreneurial side, start immediately.

One of the decisions that I did in my life that was very hard to make was opening my own business, first because I didn't have any experience as an entrepreneur for a retail store. But I also didn't have financial support, and I was single mom full of passion and very hungry. I did make it happen. It was a very difficult process, and my investment was for almost $300,000 in 2001. I worked my ass off, but at the same time, it was so worth it. I learned so many things that I carry with me today. I participated in marketing boards and business women committees, and my loan was guaranteed by a federal business agency. I was dealing with government authorities related to the international business bureau. Come on, girl, if I did it with a three-year-old baby and no husband, you can do more than that and better. I didn't have a lot of resources, but believe me, I found them!

CHAPTER 12

ACTION 9—
Who Are You Now?

This is your new way to talk about yourself. Imagine that I'm walking down the street and we see each other, and I say, "Hey, tell me about your life! I haven't seen you for a while and I can tell that you look different."

What is your answer? What will it be one year from now? People are going to start noticing that you are doing something different. When you start planning your life and start seeing great results, you will feel empowered. When you finish this book, you may want to go back and start filling out all the templates or create your own and make a plan of action, lists, or start calling people. You will be *on fire!*

There is no reason why you have to stop your life's dream; make it happen! Be part of the statistics of those women who make the difference in other people's lives. Turn your world into one that is full of positivity and enthusiasm and live your best life now!

I want to dedicate a song to you from the movie *The Greatest Showman*. The song is "This Is Me" by Alan Walker Relict, sung by Keala Settle. This is my anthem! If you one day go to one of my events, you will listen to that song repeatedly. At the end you will repeat with me, "I am who I'm meant to be." Just writing that, I got goosebumps!

CHAPTER 13

ACTION 10–
Hire a Coach

Why did I hire two coaches at the same time? Before I answer, I have to say that I'm so grateful that I found my coaches. They are my inspiration; one is for my personal development and advance coaching certifications, and the second is my writing coach. Without them, my life would be completely different.

Let me explain the reason why a coach should be part of your life forever. But first, let's define what coaching is and who is a business and career coach.

What is Coaching?

Coaching is a process that helps and facilitates learning and development while allowing the client to improve their performance. It supports strengths, talents, and abilities, all while helping people overcome obstacles to reach their own goals.

What is Business Coaching?

Business coaching is a process that enhances a client's behavior and performance within the context of business. This can be with the owner of a business, managers within a business structure, or any employees who work for a business. Business coaching can also include working with a team within the framework of a business. Business coaches work with both individuals, teams, and organizations. The one-on-one coaching can be face to face or virtual.

What is a Business Coach?

They are trained coaches with a background or training in business.

Usually they have some experience in the business world—experience that can be applied when working with clients. They also:

• Help identify and clarify business goals and objectives

- Help clients look at the big picture while paying attention to the small details
- Provide candid feedback about strengths, weaknesses, progress, and obstacles
- Guide clients in gaining business knowledge and enhancing their business skills
- Listen, guide, encourage, motivate, support, and assess

A Definition of Coaching is Flexible and Evolving

Good coaches are flexible and adapt to new theories and skills. Good coaches use a process, but if you want to compete in a highly dynamic and competitive industry like business coaching, then be prepared to consistently change your business coaching definition. The foundation of your work remains the same, but you are tasked with lifelong learning and the ability to be flexible.

This is why I love my coaches, and the reason why I love to be a coach!

Conclusion

This is the best part of the book! This is because I know that if you are here with me, I'm changing one more woman's life. What an amazing milestone for both of us.

My beautiful reader, every night that I was writing to you, I was focused. I prayed to God that every word that came out of my mind was an inspiration for you and would help you on every page to wake you up and start creating curiosity. I wanted to let you know that you are not alone. You don't have to make this decision in five seconds, but you should hurry up because you have been postponing this desire for too long.

If I make a synopsis of all I have said, I will say this: you are worth it, and I believe in you and you deserve a successful life.

We are starting a new life together, because I know that you are going to relate to me forever. You must promise me that you are going to talk to your best friend and make her read this book as well, and you are going to oversee the transformation. That way the mission will never stop.

I want for a moment to talk to you about the *decision*.

Are you going to continue in the company that you are working for and climb the corporate ladder? Or are you going to make the decision and move forward to the entrepreneurial life?

What is in your heart?

My interest here is that you have resources to open your eyes and choose the better of two worlds.

I want to provide you with my experiences and alternatives that make you analyze where you are and where you are going to be. The areas that are your strength should be clear for you, before you start moving. Clarity is the key! Once you have clarity you are *free!* The structure of the actions in this book have purpose, the flow of every chapter has a reason why it is that way.

I asked you how lost you were, then I told you my story for you to know who I am, and the rest of the chapters composed ten actions where I described the way for you to follow and make your own recipe. Every ingredient that I included here is one piece of who you are. I know if you didn't find the answer you can go back and ask the questions, "Who am I? What do I want?"

My *why* does make me wake up in the morning. That is when I try to conquer the world. I want you to be strong and take each of the actions and write it down beside your bed and every day start with a different one.

Ask the questions, "Who am I and what do I want?" in each one of the actions. For example:

- **ACTION 1** is about how professional you are.
  - **The question is:** Who am I as a professional?
- **ACTION 2** is about the many hats you wear and the many stages in life.
  - **The question is:** What is my stage in life and what is my responsibility and role in it?
- **ACTION 3** is about your network and expansions.
  - **The question is:** How can I be ready to meet other people and expand my relationships?

During the last twenty years, I've been drawing hundreds of action plans for each milestone, and if you are one of my team members who is reading my book, you will remember how important it is to have *one pager* to follow up on a monthly basis and to be excellent in execution.

I am so proud of you! Thank you for reading the entire book and getting to this page. If you're here, it is because I know that you will be part of my women in action who are ready to evolve!

References

1. Anushay Hossain, "Women and Multitasking: Asset or Enemy?" *Forbes,* December 2, 2013, https://www.forbes.com/sites/worldviews/2013/12/02/women-and-multitasking-asset-or-enemy/#6e035d563bf5

2. "How Many Women Are in the World?" *Reference*,* https://www.reference.com/world-view/many-women-world-a8e6facca00d95b6

3. "leader" *Business Dictionary,* http://www.businessdictionary.com/definition/leader.html

4. "Women in Leadership," *Pew Research Center,* January 14, 2015, http://www.pewsocialtrends.org/2015/01/14/chapter-1-women-in-leadership/

5. Amy Adkins, "Only One in 10 People Possess the Talent to Manage," *Gallup*, April 13, 2015, https://www.gallup.com/workplace/236579/one-people-possess-talent-manage.aspx

6. Steve Siebold, "Interviewing over 1,200 rich people has taught me exactly how money affects the most important things in our lives," *Business Insider*, August 21, 2015, https://www.businessinsider.com/how-money-affects-the-most-important-things-in-life-2015-8

7. Melanie Greenberg Ph. D., "Is Money the Secret to Happiness?" *Psychology Today*, September 10, 2012, https://www.psychologytoday.com/us/blog/the-mindful-self-express/201209/is-money-the-secret-happiness

Acknowledgments

When you have a dream, some people are very important, especially those who support you to reach your goals in life, for their love, dedication, and understanding. I'm dedicating this book to the lights of my life. The first one is a young man who was my first love; since the moment that he was born, he has inspired me to be a better woman and a better mother. He is Sergio A. Casas, my son. The second is a beautiful princess who keeps me on my toes; she is the reason why I'm full of energy every day, she is my sunshine who always kisses me a hundred times before I go to bed. She is Mia A. Petterle, my daughter.

Evian Flores, thank you for everything that you have been doing since the first day that I said, "I'm going to write a book!" For your patience and dedication and for believing in me since the day that we met. He is one of the most important persons in my life; he is my love.

To my family: my mom, Alminda Mena; my dad, Jose Carrasco; my brother, Alexander Carrasco; and my nephew, Brandon Carrasco, for their unconditional love and support. They have been close to my heart since I was born and are a very important part of my life, and I know that no matter what I need, they always will say yes! I love each one of you to the infinite and beyond!

My friends, who always have time to listen to my projects and to be part of my story for more than twenty years, Celimar Adames and Jenniffer Pacheco are the sisters whom life gave me. I can't see my life without them. Lots of love, sisses!

To the Morgan James Publishing team: Special thanks to David Hancock, CEO & Founder for believing in me and my message. To my Author Relations Manager, Margo Toulouse, thanks for making the process seamless and easy. Many more thanks to everyone else, but especially Jim Howard, Bethany Marshall, and Nickcole Watkins.

To my coaches! Because of these two women, the last three years of my life have been turned upside down for the best. Your wisdom, inspiration, and support are part of my success today. Thank you to Gina DeVee and Dr. Angela E. Lauria—you both are amazing! This book is made by love and God, who guided me every second during this great adventure of writing.

About the Author

Ydalmis Carrasco, MBA

Ydalmis is a forward-thinking commercial operation and marketing executive with domestic and international experience in generating revenue and improving operational performance. She creates and deploys innovative sales and marketing tactics to expand market share and develop new business. She has twenty-three years of experience working in the pharmaceutical, medical device, and biologics industries on communication, commercial operations, and marketing in the United States; English, Dutch and French Caribbean; Dominican Republic; Puerto Rico; and Latin America. She leads cross-functional teams and aligns strategy to resources and employee efforts to execute company goals and establishes cost controls and robust planning procedures to promote efficiency. Ydalmis demonstrates success in marketing planning, new product launches, and field communications, all while managing forecasts, sales quotas, and budgeting to effectively lead sales performance and marketing ROI. She is a results-oriented leader with a comprehensive global and domestic experience in Fortune 500 companies.

Thank You!

Thank you for reading. For free resources and further support, please contact me at

Ydalmis@leadinglifeyc.com.

CPSIA information can be obtained
at www.ICGtesting.com
Printed in the USA
LVHW090825071219
639768LV00004B/853/P